Zz

Maria Puchol

Abdo
EL ABECEDARIO
Kids

abdopublishing.com

Published by Abdo Kids, a division of ABDO, PO Box 398166, Minneapolis, Minnesota 55439.
Copyright © 2018 by Abdo Consulting Group, Inc. International copyrights reserved in all countries.
No part of this book may be reproduced in any form without written permission from the publisher.

Printed in the United States of America, North Mankato, Minnesota.

102017

012018

 THIS BOOK CONTAINS
RECYCLED MATERIALS

Photo Credits: iStock, Shutterstock

Production Contributors: Teddy Borth, Jennie Forsberg, Grace Hansen

Design Contributors: Christina Doffing, Candice Keimig, Dorothy Toth

Publisher's Cataloging in Publication Data

Names: Puchol, Maria, author.

Title: Zz / by Maria Puchol.

Description: Minneapolis, Minnesota : Abdo Kids, 2018. | Series: El abecedario |
    Includes online resource and index.

Identifiers: LCCN 2017941885 | ISBN 9781532103261 (lib.bdg.) | ISBN 9781532103865 (ebook)

Subjects: LCSH: Alphabet--Juvenile literature. | Spanish language materials--Juvenile literature. |
    Language arts--Juvenile literature.

Classification: DDC 461.1--dc23

LC record available at https://lccn.loc.gov/2017941885

Contenido

La Zz

Zulema abra**z**a a su hermana más de una ve**z** al día.

La Zz

Los **z**orros no tienen **zarpas**,

ca**z**an sus presas saltando.

La Zz

A **Z**oe le asombra la belle**z**a de las a**z**ucenas.

La Zz

Él pasó muy velo**z** por la **z**ona de **zigzag**.

La Zz

A **Z**acarías le encanta su maestra de dan**z**a.

La Zz

Zenaida es **z**urda, escribe con la i**z**quierda.

La Zz

Ezequiel se zambulle en la piscina.

La Zz

Le duele la cabeza de pensar en la adivinanza.

La Zz

¿Qué es muy dulce y rico, pero no es sano comer mucho?

(el a**z**úcar)

Más palabras con **Zz**

panza

cerezas

zarigüeya

lanzamiento

Glosario

zarpa
mano de ciertos animales, como el león y el oso, con dedos y uñas duras.

zigzag
línea que ondula de derecha a izquierda alternativamente.

Índice

abdokids.com

¡Usa este código para entrar en abdokids.com y tener acceso a juegos, arte, videos y mucho más!

Código Abdo Kids:
EAK2998

THE TRAVELING MUSICIANS

A story by the Brothers Grimm with drawings by

HANS FISCHER

HARCOURT, BRACE & WORLD, INC.

NEW YORK

ORIGINALLY PUBLISHED IN SWITZERLAND IN 1944. PRINTED IN THE UNITED STATES OF AMERICA

THERE once was a donkey, who for many a long year had patiently carried sacks to the mill, but his strength was now failing and every day he was growing less fit for hard work. His master therefore thought he would get rid of him. But the donkey saw that some mischief was brewing, so he ran away and set out on the road to the big city, for there, he thought, he could become a musician in the town band.

When he had gone a little way he came across a hound lying by the roadside and panting as if he were tired out with running. "Why are you panting so hard, big dog?" asked the donkey. "Alas," said the dog, "because I am old and grow weaker every day, and since I cannot go hunting any more, my master wanted to kill me. So I ran away. But now how shall I earn my living?" "I'll tell you what," said the donkey. "I am going to the big city to become a musician in the town band. Come with me and join the band too. I will play the trumpet and you can beat the drum." The dog agreed, so they went on their way.

Before long they saw a cat sitting by the roadside with a face as long as three wet Sundays. "What is wrong with you, my friend?" asked the donkey. "How can I be happy when my life is in danger?" replied the cat. "Because I am growing old, my teeth are no longer sharp, and I would rather sit and purr by the fireside than chase around after mice. So my mistress wanted to drown me. It is true I was able to run away, but now I am in a fix; where am I to go?" "Come with us to the big city. You are a good night-singer, so you can be a musician in the town band." The cat thought it was a fine idea, and joined the party.

Soon afterwards the three runaways came to a farm where they saw a cock perched on the gate, crowing for all he was worth. "You deafen our ears with your screeching," said the donkey. "What are you up to?" "I told them we were going to have fine weather for the holiday," said the cock, "but because guests are coming to dinner tomorrow my mistress was hard-hearted enough to tell the cook she wanted to have me put in the soup. So my neck must be wrung tonight." "Poor old cock-a-doodle," said the donkey. "You had better come along with us. We are going to the big city. You deserve something better than to be killed. You have a fine voice, and if we give a concert it ought to be a good one."

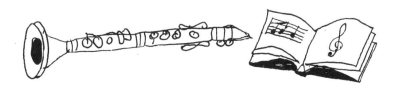

The cock was pleased with the idea, and all four of them went off together. But they could not reach the big city in one day, and in the evening they came to a wood where they decided to spend the night.

The donkey and the dog lay down under a big tree, the cat and the cock went up into the branches. The cock flew to the very top where he felt safest. Before he went to sleep he looked around in all directions and thought he saw a light burning in the distance. He called out to his companions that there must be a house not very far away as a light was shining. "We must get up and go to the house, for there is not enough shelter here," said the donkey. "Besides," said the dog, "I could do with a couple of bones with some meat on them." So off they set in the direction of the light, and soon they saw it shining brighter and bigger. At last they came to a brightly-lit house in which a gang of robbers lived. The donkey, being the tallest, went up to the window and peeped in.

"What do you see?" asked the cock. "What do I see?" the donkey replied. "A table full of good things to eat and drink, and robbers sitting round it enjoying themselves." "That would just suit us," said the cock. "Yes indeed, if we could only get in," said the donkey. So the animals discussed what they should do to get rid of the robbers, and at last they hit upon a plan. The donkey was to stand by the window ledge, the dog was to stand on the donkey's back, the cat was to climb on top of the dog, and lastly the cock was to fly up and perch on the cat's head. When all was ready, they started their music. The donkey brayed, the dog barked, the cat miauwed, and the cock crowed. Then they plunged through the window amidst a clatter of broken glass.

The robbers sprang up at the dreadful din, thinking it must be some terrible hobgoblin, and fled into the wood in a great fright. Then the four friends sat down at the table, greedily snatching what was left, and eating as though they feared they were going to starve for the next month.

When the four friends had finished they put out the light

and went to find a place to sleep, each to his own taste.

The donkey lay down on the rubbish heap, the dog behind the door, the cat on the hearth by the fireside, while the cock perched on the roof. And as they were tired out after their long journey they soon fell asleep. When it was past midnight the robbers saw from afar that all the lights were out in the house, and since everything seemed to be quiet, the robber chief said: "We really should not have let ourselves be scared. Someone must go and search the house." The robber who was sent found everything quiet, so he went into the kitchen to light a candle. Thinking the bright eyes of the cat were glowing coals, he held a match to them to light it.

But the cat did not take this as a joke. It sprang at the robber's face, spat at him and scratched him. He shrank back in a great fright and made for the door, but the dog, which was lying there, jumped up and bit him in the leg. And as he ran out into the courtyard past the rubbish heap, the donkey gave him a powerful kick with its hind leg, while the cock, awakened by the noise, crowed from the roof, "Cock-a-doodle-doo." So the robber ran as fast as he could back to his chief and said: "Oh, there is a dreadful witch in the house. She breathed on me and scratched my face with her long finger nails. And in front of the door there stands a man with a knife. He stabbed me in the leg. And in the courtyard there is a black monster which hit me with a club. And up on the roof is sitting the devil, and he called out: 'Bring the rascal here.' So I made off."

After this the robbers dared not go near the house again, and the four traveling musicians were so happy that they never wanted to leave it. And they may still be there to this very day.